Nightmares of Nature

Ian Rohr

sundance™

Published by
Sundance Publishing, LLC
33 Boston Post Road West
Suite 440
Marlborough, MA 01752
800-343-8204
www.sundancepub.com

First published 2002 by
Blake Education, Locked Bag 2022, Glebe 2037, Australia
Exclusive United States Distribution: Sundance Publishing

Design by Cliff Watt in association with
Sundance Publishing

Nightmares of Nature
ISBN: 978-0-7608-6697-9

Photo Credits:
p. 6–9 photolibrary.com; p. 11 (top) Auscape, (bottom right and left)
APL/Corbis;   p. 14 (bottom) photolibrary.com; p. 15 (bottom) photolibrary.com;
p. 18 (bottom) APL/Corbis; p. 19 (top) Auscape; p. 23 (bottom) APL/Corbis.

Printed in China

10/09-225542

Table of Contents

4

Tiny Attackers

Imagine a tiny creature that can crawl up a cow's nose while she is peacefully eating grass.

The creature starts sucking the cow's blood. It grows so big on the blood that the cow's air supply is blocked off, and she dies. Such a tiny creature does exist. It's called a leech. Grazing animals, such as cattle, are the ones in danger—not us. Even so, the thought of leeches makes most of us squirm.

What creatures in nature give you nightmares? Giant spiders? Crawly things that sometimes live on our heads? There are a lot of little horrors around us, including some that bite or sting. Some are just bothersome, but others can kill. Let's have a closer look at some of nature's mini-monsters. And remember to open your eyes and watch your step!

Bloodsuckers!

There are creatures out there that want your blood, and they are well designed to just come and get it.

Hanging On Like a Leech

Leeches live everywhere, from deserts to polar regions. And some do like to suck on human blood. The bite is painless, so you probably won't even know it's latched on to you. A leech busily sucks out ten times its own weight in blood, growing up to five times bigger until it's full. Fat on your blood, it drops off and can now live for months before it must feed again.

The largest leech is the giant Amazon leech. This one is just a baby—they can grow to 46 cm (18 in.) long!

This magnified mouth of a leech has three rows of teeth to cut a Y shape in its victim. The skin at the wound then peels back and the blood flows out.

This Is Lousy!

Head feeling itchy? A bit scratchy? If so, you might be one of the millions of people who have become a home for head lice. Like leeches, lice are **parasites**. Head lice live on our heads and off our blood. Sometimes the only way to get rid of them is to shave your head!

Still can't get rid of these humans!

Magnified head louse and egg clinging to a human hair. One female can lay between 80 and 100 eggs, called nits.

Itsy-Bitsy, but Mighty Nasty

Do sticky webs and eight hairy legs make you scream? You're not alone. Fear of spiders is common. Most people don't need to have had a bad experience to still be very afraid of them.

ONE BIG SPIDER!

The venom of the hairy Goliath bird-eating spider is not very poisonous. And its bite is said not to hurt any more than a needle does. This huge spider is found in the rain forest of South America. It makes up for its lack of danger with its size and don't-mess-with-me appearance. It is big enough to wrap itself and its fangs around your face. If you put one of these 25-centimeter (10 in.) creatures on your plate, there won't be room for vegetables!

Nasty Surprises

Does walking into a web have you clawing frantically at your face to avoid a spider? If so, be careful if you're ever in a tropical forest. Orb-web spiders weave webs that can stretch 6 meters (about 20 ft.) from the treetops to the ground and measure 2 meters (7 ft.) around. And the silk spun by the female golden orb-web spider is, weight for weight, stronger than steel. The webs are strong enough to catch and hold a bird. Local people even use the webs to make fishing nets and animal traps.

Not spiders again!

This black and yellow spider is a type of orb-web spider. It has caught a hummingbird for dinner.

This female golden orb-web spider is spinning silk. Scientists are studying the silk to try to make fibers that are just as strong.

Silk

Spinneret

Deadlier Than Most

Most spiders curl up and play dead or scuttle away if they're disturbed. But the Brazilian wandering spider will stand and fight. People pushing them away with sticks or brooms are horrified when the spiders run up the handle and bite them. These spiders bite thousands of people each year. Their bite can kill a child.

Male funnel-web spiders aren't big, but with fangs that can pierce fingernails and attitude to spare, they're bad! These aggressive spiders are found in eastern Australia, and they aren't at all afraid of attacking a human. Their **venom** produces immediate, severe pain, followed by extreme sweating, muscle spasms, and cramps all through the body. If the bite is bad enough, the victim needs to quickly receive medical help. Otherwise, he or she will fall into a coma and die.

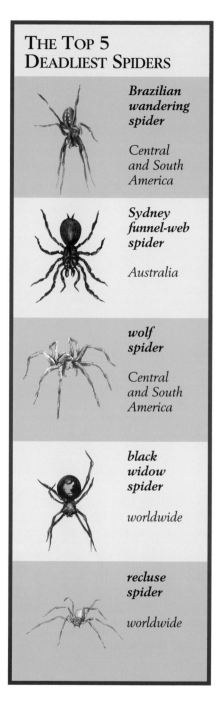

THE TOP 5
DEADLIEST SPIDERS

Brazilian wandering spider

Central and South America

Sydney funnel-web spider

Australia

wolf spider

Central and South America

black widow spider

worldwide

recluse spider

worldwide

The funnel-web spider raises its head to attack, then stabs its prey by moving its head down.

This funnel-web spider is being milked for its venom. The venom will be used to make antivenin to give to people bitten by the spiders.

Wandering spiders do not build a web. They actively hunt their prey on the forest floor.

SSSSnakes

Would you get into a bathtub full of rattlesnakes? Would you do it to set a world record?

In 1999, two American snake handlers filled two tubs with 75 western diamondback rattlesnakes each . . . and then climbed in themselves. They stayed there for ten seconds—and set a new world record. They must have known what they were doing, though, because they didn't get bitten.

For most people, this would be their worst nightmare. For thousands of years, many people have feared, hated, and killed snakes. Snakes live on every continent in the world, except Antarctica. But most people would not even consider going near a snake as dangerous as the rattlesnake.

Taking a Bite

Our horror of snakes far outweighs any real threat most of them pose to us. But some snakes have two sharp fangs full of venom and a mouth made to swallow dinner whole. So fear of certain snakes is smart!

The taipan is one of the world's deadliest snakes.

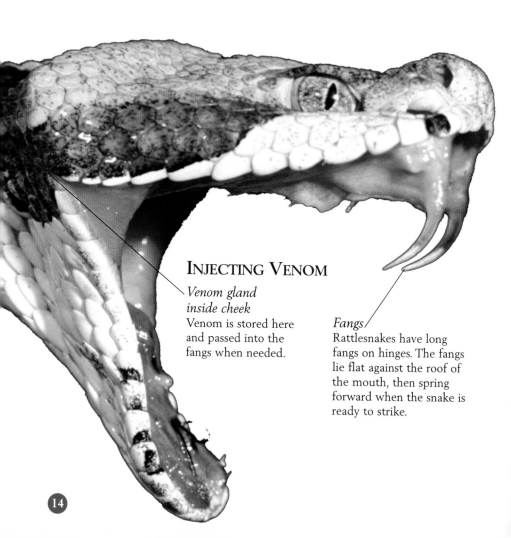

INJECTING VENOM

Venom gland inside cheek
Venom is stored here and passed into the fangs when needed.

Fangs
Rattlesnakes have long fangs on hinges. The fangs lie flat against the roof of the mouth, then spring forward when the snake is ready to strike.

Fancy Fangs

Some of the deadliest snakes have long **fangs** at the front of their mouths. They use these fangs to inject venom into their prey. The liquid is released from the venom glands when the snake bites. It then travels down the hollow fangs into the victim. These snakes are the most dangerous to humans. The long fangs pierce skin and inject venom directly into a person's bloodstream. The Gaboon viper from tropical Africa has the longest fangs. It can inject poison up to 50 millimeters (2 in.) under the skin!

The tiger snake is very aggressive. It kills more people in Australia than any other snake.

Deadly snakes, like this taipan, are milked to help produce antivenin.

Here Comes Dinner—Gulp!

Snakes with venom use it to stop prey from struggling so they can then gulp it down—in one piece. One type of venom **paralyzes** the victim by attacking its **nervous system**. Another type works by destroying the victim's muscles. Even if the prey does manage to get away, the venom still does its work. The snake just follows the animal's heat trail and finds its meal.

Most snakes have flexible mouths and jaws that can stretch to swallow animals larger than themselves. Depending on the size of the snake, a snake's diet may include insects, rats, frogs, other reptiles, and even pigs or goats. Some frogs try to defend themselves by **inflating** their mouths with air. But snakes just grab them from behind and push all the air out of the frog's mouth.

Burp!

Snakes usually eat their prey headfirst so the legs don't stick in their throat.

WHY DON'T SNAKES CHOKE?

If you ate a large piece of food and didn't chew it properly, it could get caught in your throat. Then you might choke. Snakes don't have this problem. When their mouths stretch, the position of their windpipe shifts. So a snake can still breathe even when its mouth seems filled with a whole animal.

ELASTIC JAWS

Elastic connection

Windpipe

Lower jaw

But a surprise attack from behind works best when frogs are on the menu.

Not So Tight!

Not all snakes use venom to kill their prey—some just squeeze it, and dinner is ready.

Boa constrictor

Last Breath

A lightning-fast ambush from the bushes or the water is how the South American anaconda first grabs its prey. It latches on with sharp teeth and then wraps itself around and around its victim. The prey does the rest of the work. Each time the prey breathes out, the anaconda tightens its grip. Soon, usually within a few minutes, the snake is wrapped so tightly around it that breathing becomes impossible for the victim and it **suffocates**. Pythons and boa constrictors also squeeze their prey to death.

A boa constrictor squeezes its body around a rat to kill it.

This 4.5 m (15 ft.) anaconda has a stomach bulging with dinner.

Big Feed

The anaconda uncoils itself when it is sure that its prey is dead. Then it locates the head with its flickering tongue and begins the long slow process of swallowing and digesting. It may take days for the snake to digest a pig or goat, but it won't need to eat again for up to a month.

Ooops! I've got a grip on myself.

A SENSE OF SIZE

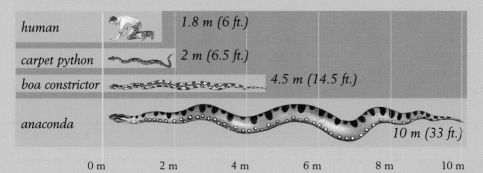

human		1.8 m (6 ft.)
carpet python		2 m (6.5 ft.)
boa constrictor		4.5 m (14.5 ft.)
anaconda		10 m (33 ft.)

0 m   2 m   4 m   6 m   8 m   10 m

First One in the Water . . . Is Dinner

Whatever you do, don't put your hand in a tank of piranha!

These little fish have sharp teeth and bad reputations. There is no proof that they really strip humans to the bone in seconds. But if it ever has happened, then the red-bellied piranha did it. When the lagoons of the Amazon River shrink in the dry season, these piranha break their usual diet of smaller fish. They'll eat anything that falls in the water.

Perhaps piranha are not quite the bad guys people think they are. But there are plenty of other nightmares waiting just below the surface. Come on in, the water's fine . . .

Hidden Dangers

When splashing around in the ocean, it pays to keep an eye out for creatures hidden in the rocks—and creatures that look like rocks!

An Eel Meal

A moray eel hovers in the water near its hole, its teeth exposed. It waits for food to swim within reach. When an unfortunate victim comes near, the eel shoots forward, grabs it, and wraps itself around it. The eel contracts its muscles from tail to head in a sudden **spasm**. Then it whips its head around, tearing off a big hunk of its victim's flesh. But, a moray eel can be as shy as it is savage. It will retreat into its hole when something that scares it comes along.

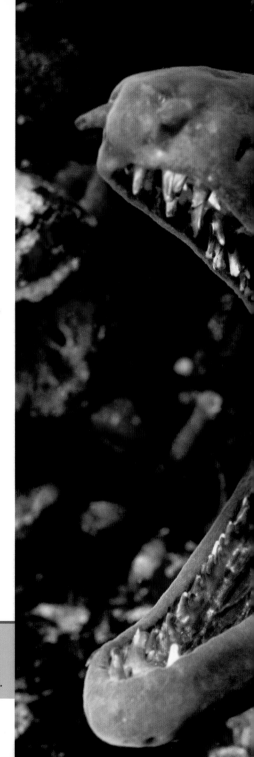

The ever-open mouth of the moray eel makes it look fierce. But the eel keeps its mouth open so water will pass over its gills, and it can breathe.

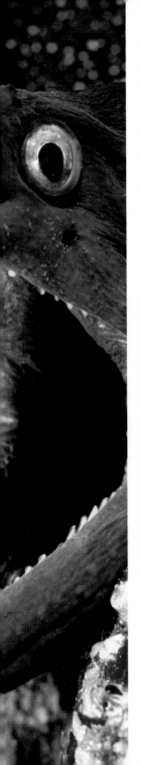

In some places, people and eels regularly cross paths. Divers have trained eels to eat from their hands and be stroked like big underwater pets. The trouble is, the eels get used to the free lunches. Then, when the hands are empty, the eels try to eat the hands instead.

Divers need to be careful not to provoke an attack from a hungry eel!

Don't Step on This Stone

For something that doesn't want to be noticed, the stonefish does have a pointed way of making its presence felt. The stonefish relies on **camouflage** and staying still to keep safe. But it has a weapon ready if anything does get too close. Lined up along its back are 13 hard, strong spines, each connected to a venom sac. If anything puts pressure on these spines, the stonefish injects its venom.

Can you find the stonefish?

The first symptom of a stonefish sting is incredible pain in the region of the wound. The agony is so intense that victims can go into immediate shock. They have even been known to bite or attack people trying to help them. When the pain stops, and this can take days, there are other problems. Symptoms such as anxiety, depression, weakness, **insomnia**, and poor concentration can last for months.

Stonefish live in the Indian and Pacific Oceans—north to China, east to Hawaii, and south to Australia.

WHAT'S A DEADLY JELLY?

The box jellyfish is one of the most poisonous creatures on Earth. Its 60 tentacles can trail up to 3 meters (10 ft.) behind its body. Each tentacle contains millions of venom-loaded capsules. These trailing tentacles can wrap around a person, resulting in widespread stinging. Beyond the physical pain, the stings can leave terrible, lifelong scarring. And that's if you're lucky. Each box jellyfish carries enough venom to kill several adult humans. This creature lives in the tropical Australian and Pacific waters.

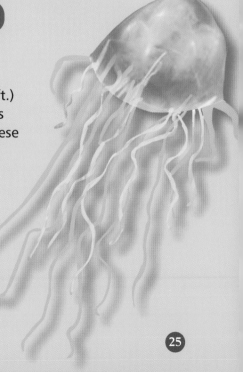

Open Wide

If you see these jaws headed your way, you had better hope it's a nightmare, and not real!

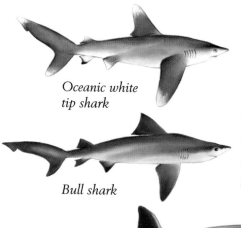

Oceanic white tip shark

Bull shark

Great white shark

Tiger shark

Surrounded by Sharks

Every year, humans kill about 100 million sharks. On the other hand, sharks attack about 50 to 75 people each year. Only about 5 to 10 of these attacks result in death. But for those people who are fatally attacked by sharks, it is a terrifying way to die.

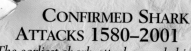

CONFIRMED SHARK ATTACKS 1580–2001

The earliest shark attack recorded in the International Shark Attack File happened in 1580.

Asia 120 57

Australia
323 149   58 8

New Zealand

Of the 400 or so known **species** of shark, only 30 have been known to attack humans. And only the tiger, great white, bull, and oceanic white tip sharks are regularly responsible for attacks on humans.

For 900 sailors who survived the sinking of the *USS Indianapolis* in 1945, this terror became real. The ship had sunk just after midnight in the deep waters of the Pacific Ocean. At sunrise, the shark attacks began. The men clung together in groups in life vests hitting at the water and kicking their feet to try to **repel** the sharks. By the time help arrived, nearly 5 days later, only 317 men had survived. Even as the men were being pulled from the sea, sharks continued to circle and strike.

Sharks are able to detect movement and even tiny amounts of blood in the murkiest water conditions.

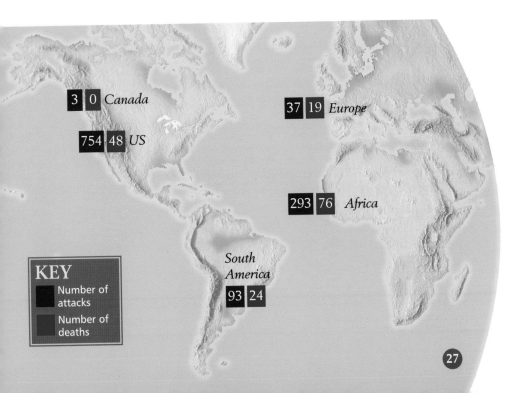

3 0 *Canada*

37 19 *Europe*

754 48 *US*

293 76 *Africa*

KEY
■ Number of attacks
■ Number of deaths

South America

93 24

Crocodiles have been around for about 240 million years. But of the 23 species of crocodiles alive today, only two are regular people killers: the Nile crocodile and the saltwater crocodile.

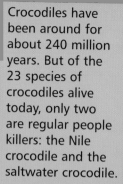

Saltwater crocodile

Stick, Rock, Crocodile?

Crocodiles live in knee-deep water and their camouflage makes them hard to see among the rocks and weeds. They will remain motionless for hours until they suddenly attack. They can hurtle themselves up to 10 meters (33 ft.) up the riverbank or 2 meters (7 ft.) straight up into the air. Then they grab their prey and drag it back to the water to be drowned, shaken to bits, and eaten.

Screams Across the Swamp

In 1945, the saltwater crocodile was responsible for one of the most nightmarish encounters recorded between humans and animals. World War II was drawing to a close. A thousand Japanese soldiers were attempting a nighttime retreat across a thick, dark swamp between Burma and Romree Island. Nearby Allied troops listened in horror to the terrible screams and gunshots as the crocodiles attacked the Japanese soldiers. By daybreak only about 20 of the soldiers were still alive.

Crocodile teeth can only grip, not chew. Crocodiles swallow prey whole or shake it into bite-sized pieces.

A horrible real-life nightmare!

Fact File

From Nightmares . . . to Phobias

zoophobia

ZO-A-FO-BEE-A

Fear of animals

arachnophobia

A-RACK-NA-FO-BEE-A

Fear of spiders

ophidiophobia

O-FID-EE-A-FO-BEE-A

Fear of snakes

cynophobia

SIGH-NA-FO-BEE-A

Fear of dogs

ailurophobia

EYE-LOO-RA-FO-BEE-A

Fear of cats

ornithophobia

OR-NI-THA-FO-BEE-A

Fear of birds

alektrophobia

A-LECK-TRA-FO-BEE-A

Fear of chickens

entomophobia

EN-TA-MO-FO-BEE-A

Fear of insects

saurophobia

SAW-RA-FO-BEE-A

Fear of lizards

Glossary

camouflage a disguise, usually a creature's markings or skin color, that helps it to blend into its environment

fangs long, sharp teeth through which venom is injected into a victim

inflating puffing up, expanding, or swelling

insomnia inability to sleep

nervous system system of nerves throughout an animal's or human's body

paralyzes makes unable to move

parasites animals or plants that live on or in another animal or plant

repel to drive away or force back

spasm a sudden muscle contraction

species a group of animals or plants with similar characteristics or qualities

suffocates dies because it can't get enough air

venom poisonous fluid that animals, including spiders and snakes, inject into their prey

Inflating

Index